THE RESTORATION OF 4 EZRA (2 ESDRAS) RECOVERED FOR THE REMNANT

*A Faithful Reconstruction of
YHWH's Word
Based on Surviving Manuscripts*

Sahar Soltani

Copyright © 2025 Sahar Soltani
All rights reserved.

This restoration is part of the Sacred Writings project dedicated to recovering the unaltered Word of YHWH.
No part of this publication may be reproduced, stored in a retrieval system, or transmitted in any form, electronic, mechanical, photocopying, recording, or otherwise, without prior written permission from the author, except for brief quotations used in reviews, articles, or scholarly works.

Disclaimer:
This is a restoration, not a reinterpretation. Every effort has been made to remain faithful to the original intent of the sacred text, with restored Divine Names and original structure preserved. This work does not reflect any denomination, creed, or tradition, but solely aims to recover the purity of YHWH's Word based on surviving manuscripts. It is offered with reverence, not authority. No human ownership is claimed over the Word of YHWH.

Published by The Quiet Seer Press, Toronto, Canada
Restored, formatted, and designed by Sahar Soltani

Email: quietseerpress@outlook.com
For inquiries regarding this publication and other Sacred Writings projects.

Printed and distributed globally via independent publishing services and retail networks.
First Edition 2025
ISBN: 9781069554789

Restoration Note

This is a word-for-word restoration of the Sacred Writings, based on the earliest surviving manuscripts and interlinear sources, with divine names, YHWH, Yeshua and Ruach, restored in reverence.

Every effort has been made to preserve the original intent, structure, and theological meaning without injecting modern interpretation, doctrine, or opinion. Formatting has been applied only for clarity and poetic flow, never to alter the message.

This restoration removes later insertions, mistranslations, and doctrinal tampering that have obscured the identity of Yeshua as YHWH and erased the divine Name. It seeks not to add, but to return to the unaltered breath of the Word as it was given.

This is not a new translation. It is a careful recovery of a scroll that was once honored by many believers before being cast aside, not by divine decree, but by men.

4 Ezra, also known as 2 Esdras, contains deep prophetic truth about the end times, divine justice, the agony of the righteous, and the hidden mysteries given to Ezra after the destruction of the Second Temple.

This restoration is not grounded in any denomination's approval or man-made canon, but in:

- A comparison of the oldest surviving manuscripts (Latin, Syriac, Ethiopic),
- A restoration of divine Names and Hebrew thought patterns,
- And above all, a return to the Spirit of YHWH who still speaks through His remnant.

This restoration has been prayerfully discerned, not blindly accepted. Where lines appeared corrupted or later inserted, they were identified during the restoration process and addressed in alignment with the earliest witnesses. No annotations are included here, for the text is presented whole. Everything hidden has been brought into the light. This is a recovery, not a reinvention.

No human tradition, denomination, or institution is represented here. This is not a translation. This is not a commentary. This is a **restoration.**

All who read are urged to test every word, with humility and awe, before the presence of YHWH Himself.

The aim is not to lead anyone away from Scripture, but deeper into it, cleaner, bolder and free of the filters imposed by empires, councils, and corrupted systems.

As the Bereans did (Acts 17:11), you are invited to examine everything and return to the voice of the Most High (El Elyon).

May this restored scroll feed the hungry, awaken the sleeping, and strengthen the faithful.

Transparency Notes

This restoration has been prepared with full transparency so that every reader may discern its integrity for themselves.

Manuscripts Used
- The Latin Codex Sangermanensis and related textual witnesses.
- Surviving Syriac and Ethiopic versions.
- Comparative use of interlinear and concordance-based sources.

Restored Names
- **YHWH (יהוה)**: Restored wherever the covenant Name was obscured or replaced (commonly as "LORD" or "GOD"). This is the personal Name of the Most High.
- **Elohim (אֱלֹהִים)**: Preserved wherever the manuscripts use it, whether for the true Elohim, false gods, or mighty beings, according to context.
- **Yeshua (ישוע)**: Preserved as the revealed identity of YHWH in the flesh.
- **Ruach (רוּחַ)**: Used for the Spirit of YHWH.
- **Why both YHWH and Elohim are kept**: To collapse everything into one word would distort the original witness. Elohim expresses might and

category, while YHWH reveals covenant identity. Both are essential to preserve the meaning given by the Spirit through the prophets.

Approach Taken

- Where tampering, insertions, or doctrinal influences were suspected, those lines were deliberately excluded to preserve the integrity of the original text.
- Formatting has been applied for poetic flow and readability but never to alter meaning.
- No denominational authority or tradition has been followed. The only measure has been fidelity to the earliest surviving witnesses and to the Spirit of YHWH.

Transparency About Tools

Modern tools, including AI, were employed to compare manuscripts side-by-side, flag later insertions, and assist in drafting consistent line formatting.

These tools are instruments only, never authorities.

Why Transparency Matters

The purpose of this work is not to claim authority, but to provide clarity. No human ownership is claimed over the Word of YHWH. Readers are invited to test every word, as the Bereans did (Acts 17:11), to weigh what has been restored, and to discern in reverence before the Most High.

Where Latin manuscripts reflected obvious replacement of the divine Name (Dominus, Deus), this restoration returns to **YHWH** and **Elohim** according to Hebraic context, with confirmation from Syriac and Ethiopic witnesses where possible.

x

Preface: Why This Restoration Begins at Chapter 3 and Ends at Chapter 14

The book commonly known as 2 Esdras or 4 Ezra has survived in three sections:
- Chapters 1–2 (often labeled 5 Ezra)
- Chapters 3–14 (the authentic 4 Ezra)
- Chapters 15–16 (often labeled 6 Ezra)

Only Chapters 3–14 are found in the earliest and most reliable manuscripts (Latin, Syriac, Ethiopic). The opening (1–2) and the closing (15–16) appear centuries later and were absent from the earliest textual witnesses.

Why 1–2 Are Excluded
- These chapters are a later Christian addition, written in a different style, with content that reflects much later concerns.
- Even scholars who defend their inclusion acknowledge they are not part of the original Ezra scroll.
- They were inserted to frame Ezra's visions in a way that better fit institutional theology.

Why 15–16 Are Excluded
- These chapters are also absent from the oldest manuscripts.

- Their style and vocabulary differ significantly from the authentic core (3–14).
- Many experts agree they were written much later and attached as an apocalyptic appendix.

Why 3–14 Are Preserved
- These chapters form a complete, unified narrative: Ezra's laments, angelic dialogues, visions, and revelations after the destruction of the Second Temple.
- They have consistent style, theology, and structure, unlike the additions.
- Even within the scholarly world, "4 Ezra" = chapters 3–14.

And as we have all labored to understand how Ezra came to write these visions, it must be remembered: Ezra did not invent, nor imagine nor later comment upon these writings. They were given directly from YHWH, through His messenger Uriel, in the days following the destruction of the Second Temple. What survives in chapters 3-14 is not man's speculation, but a sacred record of divine dialogue, entrusted to Ezra the scribe, and preserved for the remnant by El Elyon, the Most High.

Why This Matters
This restoration does not remove content out of personal preference or denominational bias. Instead, it honors the

true heart of Ezra's revelation, uncluttered by later hands.

To include 1–2 and 15–16 would be to knowingly mix later writings with the authentic scroll. To focus on 3–14 is to let the original voice of Ezra and YHWH speaking through him be heard in its integrity.

For clarity: this restoration does not deny the existence of chapters 1–2 and 15–16 in later traditions. They are acknowledged, but not included, because they are absent from the oldest manuscript witnesses and bear the marks of later composition. To present them as equal with Ezra's true visions would be to mingle man's words with YHWH's revelation. This restoration seeks only to guard the purity of what was given. To mix later additions with what YHWH gave through Ezra would not only obscure the original vision but would violate the command not to add to His Word (*see* Deuteronomy 4:2). This restoration seeks to guard the sacred boundary between what is divine and what is human.

To Those Who Remain

This restoration was appointed for you.
To the ones who will open these pages
when the world is shaking
and nothing feels safe anymore.

If you are reading this after the trumpet has sounded,
and the called and faithful have been taken,
know this:

**YHWH let this book survive
so you could hold it now.**

This is not a coincidence.
This is mercy.

These words were given to Ezra
after the fall of the Temple,
and they were preserved,
and perhaps restored for this very season,
when the systems of man have collapsed,
and the churches and their buildings,
built on dust, have fallen.

Be one of the *Ekklesia*, the called-out ones:
not a pew-sitter,
not a follower of pagan calendars

or man-made traditions.

Seek His Word in its Original Writing,
the Word as it was first given,
not the versions reshaped by councils or creeds,
not filtered through doctrines and interpretations
shaped by men,
culture or compromise.

Rise Up, Ekklesia!
Rise Up, Remnant!

Take up your armor.
Wait with strength.
Hold fast for the Great Day of our Creator,
the Righteous Judge,
the Almighty Warrior,
the Ruler of this universe,

YHWH Yeshua!

May the power of the One True Elohim rest upon you.
May you be filled, as they were in the upper room, with
the fire of His Ruach.
Go forth as soldiers of YHWH:
casting out demons,
healing the broken,
speaking with fire,
standing unshaken as the darkness rages.

For as great as the shaking will be,
greater still will be the outpouring of His Spirit
upon all who call on His Name.

Table of Contents

Restoration Note…………………………….……..….iii
Transparency Notes…………………………………..…vi
Preface: Why This Restoration Begins at Chapter 3 and Ends at Chapter 14……………………….……………..xi
Dedication: To Those Who Remain…………………..xv

The Restoration of 4 Ezra (2 Esdras 3–14)
Chapter 3……………………………………………………….3
Chapter 4……………………………………………………….9
Chapter 5…………………………………………………...17
Chapter 6……………..………………………………………23
Chapter 7………………………………………………….33
Chapter 8…………………………………………………...47
Chapter 9…………………………………………………….57
Chapter 10…………………………………………………….65
Chapter 11…………………………………………………….75
Chapter 12…………………………………………………….81
Chapter 13…………………………………………………….87
Chapter 14…………………………………………………….97

Appendix Notes: Key Terms & Images in Ezra………105
Glossary of Names and Terms in 4 Ezra (2 Esdras 3-14)... ………………………………………………………….109
References & Sources………………………………….113
About the Sacred Writings Restoration Project………117

The Restoration of 4 Ezra (2 Esdras) Chapters 3–14

4 Ezra (2 Esdras) – Chapter 3

1 In the thirtieth year after the ruin of the city,
I, Ezra, was in Babylon, and lay troubled upon my bed,
and my thoughts came up over my heart:

2 For I saw the desolation of Tsion,
and the wealth of those who dwelt at Babylon.

3 And my spirit was deeply moved,
so that I began to speak words full of fear to Elyon,
and said,

4 "O Adonai YHWH,
You spoke at the beginning,
when You planted the earth,
and that alone, without help,
and commanded the dust,

5 And it gave You Adam,
a lifeless body.
Yet he was the workmanship of Your hands,
and You breathed into him the breath of life,
and he was made alive before You.

6 And You led him into the garden,
which Your right hand had planted,
before the earth came forward.

7 And You laid upon him one commandment:
but he transgressed it,
and immediately You appointed death for him,
and in him there sprang up generations,
nations, peoples, and kindreds, out of number.

8 And to him You gave commandment
to love Your way,
and You appointed him life,
and You gave him a law,
yet he transgressed it.

9 And immediately You appointed death for him
and for his generations,
from whom were born nations,
tribes, peoples, and kindreds without number.

10 And every one of them walked after their own will,
and did ungodly things before You,
and scorned You.

11 And You did not hinder them.

12 But again in process of time
You brought the flood upon those
that dwelt in the world,
and destroyed them.

13 And the same fate befell them;
as Adam had transgressed,
they also who were born of him.

14 And You did leave one of them, Noah,
with his household, and all the righteous
that came of him.

15 And it happened,
when those that dwelt upon the earth began to multiply,
and had begotten many children,
and were a great people,
they began again to be more ungodly than the first.

16 Now when they lived so wickedly before You,
You chose a man from among them,
whose name was Abraham.

17 Him You loved,
and to him only You showed Your will.

18 And made an everlasting covenant with him,
promising him that You would never forsake his seed.

19 And You gave him Yitsḥaq,
and to Yitsḥaq also You gave Yaʿaqov and Esau.
As for Yaʿaqov, You chose him for Yourself,
and put by Esau:
and so Yaʿaqov became a great multitude.

20 And it happened,
when You led his seed out of Egypt,
You brought them up to Mount Sinai.

21 You bowed the heavens,
shook the earth,
moved the world,
made the depths to tremble,
and troubled the men of that age.

22 And Your glory went through the four gates of fire,
of earthquake,
of wind,
and of frost,
that You might give the Torah to the seed of Ya'aqov,
and diligence to the seed of Yisra'el.

23 Yet You did not take away from them
their wicked heart,
so that Your Torah might bring forth fruit in them.

24 For the first Adam, bearing a wicked heart,
transgressed and was overcome;
and so be all they that are born of him.

25 Thus infirmity was made permanent;
and the Torah also in the heart of the people
with the malignity of the root;

so that the good departed away,
and the evil abode still.

26 So the times passed away,
and the years were brought to an end:
then did You raise up for Yourself a servant, David.

27 Whom You commanded to build a city
to Your Name,
and to offer incense and oblations to You there.

28 When this was done many years,
then they that inhabited the city forsook You,

29 And in all things did even as Adam and all his
generations had done:
for they also had a wicked heart.

30 And so You gave the city over
into the hands of Your enemies.

31 Are their deeds then any better that inhabit Babylon,
that they should therefore have the dominion
over Tsion?

32 For when I came here,
and had seen impieties without number,
then my soul saw many evildoers in this thirtieth year,
so that my heart failed me.

33 For I have seen how You suffer them sinning,
and have spared wicked doers,
and have destroyed Your people,
and have preserved Your enemies,
and have not shown to those who love You how Your way is to be established.

34 Are the deeds of other nations then any better than those of my people,
that they should have dominion over them on the earth?
For I have gone up and seen:
they have not kept Your statutes.

35 Therefore weigh our iniquities now in the balance,
and theirs also that dwell in the world;
and so shall it be found which way is lighter.

36 And when You find them not lighter than ours,
then punish us with judgment.

4 Ezra (2 Esdras) – Chapter 4

1 And the angel that was sent to me,
whose name was Uriel,
answered,

2 and said to me:
"Your heart has gone too far in this world, Ezra,
and do you think you can grasp the way of the Most High?"

3 And I said,
"Yes, my master."
And he answered me,
"I was sent to show you three ways,
and to set forth three likenesses before you.

4 If you can declare one of them to me,
I will show you also the way that you desire to see,
and I will teach you why your heart trembles."

5 And I said,
"Speak on, my master."
And he said to me,
"Go, weigh me the weight of the fire.
Or measure me the blast of the wind.
Or call back for me the day that is past."

6 And I answered,
"Who of men can do this?
How can I answer such things?"

7 And he said to me,
"If I had asked you,
'How many dwellings are in the depths of the sea?
How many springs are in the source of the deep?
How many streams are above the firmament?
Where are the outgoings of paradise?
Where is the pathway of the garden?'

8 You might have said:
'I have never gone down into the deep,
nor yet into Sheol,
neither into heaven.

9 I have never set foot in paradise.
I do not know the ends of the world,
nor the foundations of the heavens.'

10 If then I asked such things,
and you said, 'I do not know,'
how can you not judge within yourself
the things you daily see?

11 How then can your heart grasp the way
of the Most High?
How can your mind comprehend the things

of the Eternal?

12 Men that are perishing,
how can they understand the promise of Elohim?
For this world is corrupt and weak.

13 I said: 'I beg you, my master,
if I have found favor in your sight,
show your servant by whom You visit creation.'

14 And he said to me:
'You cannot understand what is with you.
How can your vessel comprehend what is far off?

15 For how can the corrupted,
that has already decayed with age,
understand the way of the incorruptible?

16 And I answered:
'It would have been better if the earth itself
had not been made,
so man might not have come into it.'

17 And he said:
'The things that are made have their place,
and those that are created are also ordered by YHWH.

18 Do not meddle with the affairs of the Most High.
Do not hasten with your heart above the Most High.

19 For you have seen many,
and are eager for many,
but your spirit has not been trained to weigh the times.'

20 Then I said:
'Master, I beseech you:
will I live until that day?
Or who will be alive in those times?'

21 And he answered me,
'Concerning the signs I have told you before.
At the end:
The beginning of tribulations.
The great shaking of the earth.
The failing of men.
The wavering of powers.
The fear of all that dwell on the earth.

22 The way of truth will be hidden,
and the land will be barren of faith.

23 Iniquity will be multiplied beyond what you now see,
beyond what you have heard of long ago.

24 The land will be laid waste,
and men will hate one another.

25 Cities will be in confusion.

The pride of the strong will fall.
The rulers will be troubled.

26 Men will take counsel to make war one against another,
city against city,
place against place,
people against people,
kingdom against kingdom.

27 The signs I told you before will appear,
and when they come to pass,
then my Son will be revealed,
whom you saw as a man rising.

28 When all the nations hear His voice,
every man will leave his own land,
and war will cease in the face of His appearing.

29 A gathering together will be in judgment,
and Mount Tzion will be manifest,
prepared and built,
as you saw the mountain carved without hands.

30 And my Son will reprove the nations
for their wickedness,
their wrong thoughts,
and their torments with which they afflicted.

31 He will set before them living torments,
when He rebukes them.

32 He will destroy them without labor by the Law,
which is like fire.'

33 And I said:
'Master, show me why I saw the man rising from the
heart of the sea.'

34 And He said to me:
'As no one can search or know what is in the deep
of the sea,
so none on earth can see My Son,
nor those who are with Him,
except in the time of His day.

35 This is the interpretation of the dream you saw.
You alone are enlightened in this,
for you have forsaken your own ways,
and applied yourself to Mine,
and have searched after My Torah.

36 You have ordered your life with wisdom,
and called understanding your mother.

37 Therefore I have shown you these things,
for there is a reward laid up with the Most High.
It will be after many days.'

38 And I said:
'Master, show me yet,
whether more remains behind than what has come.
For what has passed is more than what is present,
and what is to come is far beyond both.'

39 And He answered me:
'The harvest of this age is already prepared,
but the reapers are not yet ready.
For strong is the storehouse,
and the angels wait.

Yet the Head of the age commands them
not to open until the number of those who are sealed
is fulfilled.'

4 Ezra (2 Esdras) – Chapter 5

1 Nevertheless concerning the signs,
behold, the days shall come,
when those who dwell upon the earth
shall be taken in great number,
and the way of truth shall be hidden,
and the land shall be barren of belief.

2 But iniquity shall be increased
above what you now see,
or that you have heard long ago.

3 And the land that you now see ruling
shall be a wasteland,
and shall be trodden under foot by those that dwell in it.

4 For the house shall be destroyed of unrighteousness,
and sin shall be turned into it as water.

5 For the seal shall be set upon those who are to perish,
and the earth shall be left desolate and without faith.

6 But wickedness shall be increased
above what you now see,
or that you have heard long ago.

7 And it shall be that the land that you now see

to have root,
shall you see wasted suddenly.

8 But if the Most High grants you to live,
you shall see what is after the third trumpet,
that the sun shall suddenly shine again in the night,
and the moon three times in the day.

9 Blood shall drop out of wood,
and the stone shall give its voice,
and the peoples shall be troubled.

10 And he shall rule whom they look not for
who dwell upon the earth,
and the fowls shall fly away together.

11 And the Sodomitish sea shall cast out fish,
and make a noise in the night,
which many have not known,
but all shall hear its voice.

12 There shall be confusion also in many places,
and the fire shall often be sent out,
and the wild beasts shall change their places,
and women shall bring forth monsters.

13 Salt waters shall be found in the sweet,
and all friends shall destroy one another.
Then shall reason hide itself,

and wisdom shall withdraw into her secret chamber.

14 And shall be sought by many,
yet shall not be found.
Then unrighteousness and incontinency
shall be multiplied upon the earth.

15 One land also shall ask another,
and say, "Is righteousness that makes a man righteous
gone through you?"
And it shall say, "No."

16 At that time shall men hope,
and not obtain:
they shall labor,
but their ways shall not prosper.

17 These are the signs which I am permitted to tell you,
and if you pray again,
and weep as now,
and fast seven days,
you shall hear yet greater things than these.

18 Then I awoke,
and an extreme trembling went through my body,
and my soul was greatly troubled,
so that it fainted.

19 But the angel that had come and talked with me

held me, and comforted me,
and set me upon my feet.

20 And in the second night it happened,
that Phaltiel the governor of the people came to me,
saying, "Where have you been, and
why is your face so sad?

21 Do you not know that Yisra'el is committed to you in
the land of their captivity?
Rise then, and eat bread,
and forsake us not, as the shepherd that leaves his flock
in the hand of cruel wolves."

22 Then said I to him,
"Go your ways from me,
and come not near me."
And he heard what I said and went from me.

23 And so I fasted seven days, mourning and weeping,
like as Uriel the angel commanded me.

24 And after seven days the thoughts of my heart were
very grievous to me again,
and my soul recovered the spirit of understanding,
and I began to speak words full of anguish,
and said,

25 "O Adonai YHWH,

concerning all the works of Your hands,
I beg You,
show me the interpretation."

4 Ezra (2 Esdras) – Chapter 6

1 And He said to me,
"At the beginning of the circle of the earth,
before the gates of the world were fastened,
and before the winds blew,

2 Before the thunders resounded,
before lightning shone,
before foundations of Paradise were laid,

3 Before the flowers were seen,
before powers of movement were established,
before innumerable hosts of messengers were gathered,

4 Before the heights of the air were raised,
before measures of the firmaments were named,
before the footstool of Tsion was established,
before the years were numbered,
and before imaginations of those who now sin
were formed:

5 Then I considered these things,
and they were all made through Me alone,
and not through another.
As by Me also they shall be ended,
and not by another."

6 Then I answered and said,
"What shall divide the times?
Or when shall the end of the first be,
and the beginning of that which follows?"

7 And He said to me,
"From Abraham to Yitsḥaq,
when Yaaqov and Esau were born of him,
Yaʿaqov's hand first took hold of Esau's heel.

8 For Esau is the end of this age,
and Yaʿaqov is the beginning of that which follows.

9 The hand of man is between the heel and the hand;
so also are the times between."

10 Then I answered and said,
"O Adonai my Master,
if I have found favor in Your sight,

11 Show Your servant the end of Your signs,
the portion of the times that has passed,
and that which is left after."

12 And He said to me,
"Stand on your feet,
and you shall hear a mighty sound.

13 And it shall be as it were a great commotion;

but the place where you stand
shall not be moved.

14 Therefore when it speaks,
do not be afraid,
for the word concerns the end,
and the foundation of the earth is moved."

15 And I listened,
and behold, there was a great shaking,
and the place where I stood shook.

16 And I said, "O YHWH,
was this the sound of Your speaking?
And the shaking of the earth?"

17 And He said to me,
"As for what you have heard,
the sound was the beginning of the commotion
of the end.

18 The time is not yet,
when the foundations of the earth are moved,
and the portals of the world are opened,
and the steadfast above the heavens are shaken,
and the voice of the Most High is heard from the throne.

19 Then shall the channels of waters be found,
and the springs shall suddenly burst forth.

20 The woman with child shall bring forth untimely
children of three or four months,
and they shall live and not die.

21 The sudden places shall appear unsown,
the full storehouses shall suddenly be found empty.

22 And the trumpet shall give a sound,
which when every man hears,
they shall suddenly be afraid.

23 At that time shall friends fight one against another
like enemies,
and the earth shall stand in fear with those
that dwell there.
The springs of the fountains shall stand still,
and for three hours they shall not run.

24 Whoever remains from all these that I have told you
shall escape,
and see My deliverance,
and the end of your world.

25 And the men that are received
shall see it, who have not tasted death from their birth;
and the heart of the inhabitants shall be changed,
and turned into another spirit.

26 For evil shall be blotted out,
and deceit shall be quenched.

27 As for faith, it shall flourish;
corruption shall be overcome;
and the truth, which has been so long without fruit,
shall be declared."

28 And while he spoke with me,
behold, the little voice came to me, and said,

29 "Ezra, when you see that some of the signs
which I have told you come to pass,
then you shall know that it is the very time
in which Elyon will begin to visit the world
which He made."

30 And when the world shall be shaken from its places,
the speech of the Most High shall be heard,
and the earth shall quake.

31 And everyone that hears shall be afraid.

32 And then they shall see men who were taken up,
who from their birth have not tasted death;
and the heart of the inhabitants shall be turned,
and changed into another understanding.

33 For evil shall be destroyed,

deceit shall be quenched,

34 Faith shall flourish,
corruption shall be overcome,
and the truth shall be made strong."

35 Then I said,
"O YHWH,
show me yet the interpretation of this vision,
whereof I am afraid."

36 And He said to me,
"At the beginning of the circle of the earth,
before the portals of the world were fixed,
and before the winds blew,

37 Before the thunders sounded,
before lightnings flashed,
before the foundations of Paradise were laid,

38 Before the flowers were seen,
before the powers of movement were established,
before the innumerable armies of messengers
were gathered,

39 Before the heights of the air were lifted up,
before the measures of the firmaments were named,
before Tsion was prepared as a footstool:

40 Then I considered these things,
and they all were made through Me alone,
and not through another;
and by Me also they shall be ended,
and not by another."

41 Then I said,
"O Adonai,
show me the distinction between night and day."

42 And He said to me,
"Do not hasten above Elyon,
for your hastening is in vain;
did you not come into this world as one among others?

43 And your time is but short
compared with the long age to come.

44 And I answered and said,
"O Adonai,
behold, You have ordained in Your Torah that the righteous shall inherit these things,
but the wicked shall perish.

45 The righteous therefore shall suffer strait things,
and hope for wide;
but those that have done wickedly have suffered the wide things,
and shall not see the wide."

46 And He said to me,
"There is no judge above Elohim,
and none that has understanding above Elyon.

47 For there be many that perish in this life,
because they despise the Torah of Elohim that is set before them.

48 For Elohim has given a Torah to all;
and by works they shall be judged,
and by what they have done shall they be weighed."

49 Then I said,
"O Adonai,
if now You have favor upon Your servant,
show me further by whom You visit creation."

50 And He said to me,
"Concerning the coming signs,
know this first:
that in the last days the Most High will visit the inhabitants of the earth.

51 And when the earth shall quake,
the foundations be moved,
the hidden springs shall burst forth,
and the trumpet give sound,
then shall all men be afraid.

52 At that time,
friends shall fight against friends as though enemies,
and the earth shall stand in fear with those
who dwell there.

53 The fountains shall stop,
for three hours they shall not flow.

54 And whoever remains from all these that I have told you shall escape,
and see My salvation,
and the end of your world.

55 And the men that are received shall see it,
who have not tasted death from their birth;
and the heart of the inhabitants shall be changed,
and turned into another spirit.

56 For evil shall be blotted out,
deceit shall be quenched,

57 Faith shall flourish,
corruption shall be overcome,
and the truth, which has been so long without fruit,
shall be declared."

58 And while he spoke with me,
behold, little by little

the place where I stood was moved.

59 And He said to me,
"These are the signs which I have told you;
when you see them,
then know that the end is very near at hand."

4 Ezra (2 Esdras) – Chapter 7

1 And when I had finished speaking these words,
the messenger who had been sent to me before,
was sent again.

2 And he said to me,
"Rise, Ezra, and hear the words that I have come
to speak to you."

3 And I said,
"Speak on, my master."

4 Then he said to me,
"The sea is set in a wide place,
so that it might be deep and great.

5 But its entrance is narrow,
so that it must be entered through that narrow channel,
between fire on the right hand
and deep water on the left.

6 And there is only one path between them both,
even between the fire and the water,
so narrow that only one man can go upon it at once.

7 If this city now were given to a man for an inheritance,
if he never shall pass the peril set before it,

how shall he receive this inheritance?"

8 And I said,
"It is so, master."

9 Then he said to me,
"So also is Yisraʾel's portion.

10 It is prepared for you as an inheritance,
but if you will not pass through the peril set before it,
you can never take hold of that which is laid up for you."

11 And I said,
"It is so, master."

12 Then he said to me,
"Therefore YHWH Elyon has made this world for many,
but the world to come for few.

13 I will tell you a similitude, Ezra.
As when you ask the earth,
it shall say to you
that it gives much soil wherewith earthen vessels are made,
but little dust from which gold comes:
even so is the course of this present world.

14 There are many created, but few shall be saved."

15 And I answered and said,
"If I have found favor,
let me speak before You.

16 For behold, YHWH,
what about those who have been left?
Where will they be?
And what of those who were before us,
and those who are after us?"

17 And he said to me,
"The day of judgment is a crown of honor
for the righteous,
and for the ungodly it is a day of perdition.

18 The day shall be the end of this world,
and the beginning of the immortality to come,
where corruption is passed,
intemperance is at an end,
infidelity is cut off,
and righteousness is grown,
and truth is sprung up.

19 Then shall no man be able to have mercy on him who
is condemned in judgment,
nor to harm him who is victorious."

20 And I answered then and said,

"This is my first and last word:
it would have been better that the earth had not given Adam,
or else, having once given him,
to have restrained him from sinning.

21 For what good is it to all men
to live in sorrow now,
and expect punishment after death?

22 O Adam,
what have you done?
For though it was you that sinned,
the fall was not yours alone,
but ours also who come of you.

23 For what profit is it to us
if an immortal time is promised to us,
but we have done the works that bring death?

24 And if an everlasting hope has been given us,
but we have worked deeds that bring wrath?

25 And if a safe and healthy habitation has been granted us,
but we have lived wickedly?"

26 And He answered me, and said,
"This is the condition of the battle

which man that is born upon the earth shall fight:

27 That if he be overcome, he shall suffer as you have said;
but if he gets the victory, he shall receive the thing that I say.

28 For this is the life whereof Moshe spoke to the people while he lived, saying,
'Choose life, that you may live!'

29 Nevertheless they did not believe him, nor the prophets after him,
nor even Me who spoke to them.

30 That there should not be such heaviness in their destruction,
as shall be joy over those who are persuaded to salvation."

31 And I answered then and said,
"I know, Adonai,
that Elyon is called merciful,
in that He has mercy upon those who are not yet come into the world;

32 And gracious,
for He is gracious to those who turn in repentance to His Torah;

33 And patient,
for He shows patience to those who have sinned,
since they are His creatures;

34 And bountiful,
for He is ready to give rather than to take away;

35 And very compassionate,
for He multiplies mercies to those who are present,
and that are past,
and also to those who are to come.

36 For if He shall not multiply His mercies,
the world with those who dwell there would not live.

37 And if He should judge without His great mercies,
the world could not endure them that shall be judged.

38 And who could bear the weight of His judgment?
Or who is able to endure His severity?

39 O YHWH,
besides You,
there is no judge, nor any that may forgive those that sin.

40 For it is not the will of Elyon
that men should come to nothing,

but they who were created have defiled the Name of
Him that made them,
and were ungrateful to Him that prepared life for them.

41 And therefore My judgment is now at hand.

42 These things have I not showed to all men,
but to you, and a few like you."

43 Then I answered and said,
"Behold, O YHWH,
You have showed me the multitude of the wonders,
which You will begin to do in the last times:
but You have not showed me at what time."

44 And He said to me,
"Stand up upon your right side,
and I shall expound the similitude to you."

45 So I stood, and saw:
and behold, a flaming furnace passed by before me;
and it happened that when the flame had gone by,
I looked, and behold, the smoke still remained.

46 After this, there passed by before me a watery cloud,
and sent down much rain with a storm;
and when the stormy rain was past,
the drops still remained.

47 Then said He to me,
"Consider with yourself:
as the rain is more than the drops,
and as the fire is greater than the smoke,
so the measure of what is past has exceeded;
but the drops and smoke that remain are yet more than what has gone before.

48 For behold, the days shall come,
that Elyon will begin to deliver them that are upon the earth.

49 And He shall astonish the inhabitants of the world.

50 And one shall undertake to fight against another,
one city against another,
one place against another,
one people against another,
and one realm against another."

51 "For Elyon will show signs,
and wonders shall be declared.

52 The sun shall suddenly shine at night,
and the moon by day.

53 Blood shall drop out of wood,
and the stone shall give its voice,
and the peoples shall be troubled.

54 And even he shall rule,
whom they look not for that dwell upon the earth;
and the fowls shall take their flight away together.

55 And the sea of Sodom shall cast out fish,
and make a noise in the night,
which many have not known:
but they shall all hear its voice.

56 There shall be chaos also in many places,
and fire shall be sent out again,
and the wild beasts shall change their places,
and women shall bring forth monsters.

57 Salt waters shall be found in the sweet,
and all friends shall destroy one another;
then shall wisdom hide itself,
and understanding withdraw itself into its secret chamber.

58 And shall be sought of many,
and yet not be found:
then shall unrighteousness and unrest be multiplied
upon the earth.

59 One land shall also ask another,
and say, 'Is righteousness that makes a man righteous gone through you?'

And it shall say, 'No.'

60 At that time shall men hope,
and not obtain:
they shall labor, but their ways shall not prosper.

61 These signs will I show,
and afterward shall My Son be revealed,
whom You saw as a man rising up.

62 And when all the peoples hear His voice,
every man shall leave his own land and the battle they
have one against another.

63 And an innumerable multitude shall be gathered
together,
as You saw them, desiring to come,
and to overcome Him by fighting.

64 But He shall stand upon the top of Mount Tsion.

65 And Tsion shall come, and shall be shown to all men,
being prepared and built,
like as You saw the mountain carved without hands.

66 And He, My Son, shall rebuke the nations that are
come for their wickedness,
and the torments wherewith they shall be tormented.

67 And He shall destroy them without labor
by the Torah,
which is like fire.

68 And as concerning Your vision,
that You saw Him gathering to Him another peaceable multitude;

69 These are the ten tribes,
which were carried away prisoners out of their own land in the time of Hoshea the king,
whom Shalmaneser the king of Assyria led away captive,
and he carried them over the waters,
and so came they into another land.

70 But they took counsel among themselves,
that they would leave the multitude of the nations,
and go forth into a further country,
where never mankind dwelt,

71 That they might there keep their statutes,
which they never kept in their own land.

72 And they entered into Euphrates by the narrow passages of the river.

73 For Elyon then showed signs for them,
and held still the flood,

till they were passed over.

74 For through that country there was a great way to go,
namely of a year and a half:
and the same region is called Arsareth.

75 Then they dwelt there until the latter time;
and now when they shall begin to come,

76 Elyon shall stay the springs of the stream again,
that they may go through:
therefore saw You the multitude with peace.

77 But those that be left behind of Your people
are they that are found within My holy borders.

78 Now when He destroys the multitude of the nations
that are gathered together,
He shall defend His people that remain.

79 And then shall He show them great wonders."

80 Then said I,
"O YHWH Adonai,
show me this:
Why have I seen the man coming up from the midst of the sea?"

81 And He said to me,

"Like as none can seek out or know what is in the depths of the sea,
so none upon earth can see My Son, or those that are with Him,
except in that time of His day.

82 This is the interpretation of the dream which You saw,
and You alone have been enlightened about this.

83 But you have forsaken your own way,
and applied your diligence to My Torah,
and sought it out.

84 Your life you have ordered in wisdom,
and have called understanding your mother.

85 And therefore have I showed you the treasures of Elyon.
After another three days I will speak other things to you,
and declare to you mighty and wondrous things."

86 Then I went my way into the field, giving great praise and thanks to Elyon,
because of His wonders which He did in time;

87 And because He governs the same,
and such things as fall in their seasons.
And there I sat three days.

4 Ezra (2 Esdras) – Chapter 8

1 And He answered me, saying,
"The Most High has made this world for many,
but the world to come for few.

2 I will tell you a parable, Ezra:
As when you ask the earth,
and it will say to you
that it gives much clay from which earthen vessels are made,
but little dust from which gold comes:
even so is the course of this present world.

3 Many are created,
but few shall be saved."

4 So I answered and said,
"O my soul, swallow down understanding,
and devour wisdom.

5 For you have agreed to give ear,
and are willing to prophesy;
for you have no longer space than only to live.

6 O Yisra'el, if you will listen,
you shall be the crown of all,
and the Most High's beloved forever.

7 But if you will not keep the commandments,
you shall be a reproach among the nations,
and a curse among the peoples."

8 And now, Ezra,
what is it you are waiting for?
Why are you corrupting yourself
in the corruption of this age?

9 For you are weak compared to the mighty,
and you are among the feeble compared to the strong.

10 For you hasten for what is corruptible,
but you are slow for what is incorruptible.

11 You are quick for that which perishes,
but you are slow for that which is everlasting.

12 For you cannot do even what is least,
so how can you comprehend what is greater?

13 Then I answered and said,
"O my Master Adonai,
behold, You have ordained in Your Torah
that the righteous shall inherit these things,
but that the ungodly shall perish.

14 Nevertheless, the righteous shall suffer straits,

and hope for wide places;
but they that have done wickedly
have suffered the narrow
and shall not see the wide."

15 And He said to me,
"There is no judge above Elohim,
and none that has understanding above Elyon.

16 For there are many that perish in this life,
because they despise the Torah of Elohim
that is set before them.

17 For Elohim has given a plain way to all men,
to live by, if they will.

18 Nevertheless, they will not be obedient,
and speak against Him,
and imagine vain things,

19 And deceive themselves by their wicked deeds;
and they deny Elohim,
and say in their hearts, 'He is not there,'
though knowing full well they must die.

20 For the things I have said come to pass,
and shall not fail.

21 Behold, the time shall come,

that these tokens which I have told you shall come to pass,
and the bride shall appear,
and she shall be revealed,
who now is hidden from the earth.

22 And whoever is delivered from the evils I foretold
shall see My wonders.

23 For My Son shall be revealed with those that are with Him,
and those that remain shall rejoice
four hundred years.

24 After these years shall my Son the Messiah die,
and all that have the breath of man.

25 And the world shall be turned into the old silence,
seven days, like as in the former judgments,
so that no man shall remain.

26 And after seven days the world, that yet awakes not,
shall be raised up,
and that which is corrupt shall die.

27 And the earth shall restore those that sleep in her,
and the dust those that dwell in it in silence,
and the secret places shall deliver those souls
that were committed to them.

28 And Elyon shall be revealed upon the seat of judgment,
and compassion shall pass away,
and patience shall be withdrawn.

29 Only judgment shall remain,
truth shall stand,
and faith shall grow strong.

30 The work shall follow,
the reward shall be shown,
and good deeds shall awake,
and wicked deeds shall not sleep.

31 And the pit of torment shall appear,
and near it shall be the place of rest;
the furnace of Gehinnom shall be shown,
and opposite it the paradise of delight.

32 Then Elyon will say to the nations that are raised from the dead,
"Look and see whom you have denied,
whom you have not served,
whose commandments you have despised.

33 Look on this side and on that:
here is delight and rest,
and there is fire and torment."

34 Thus He shall speak to them in the day of judgment:
"This is a day that has neither sun, nor moon, nor stars,

35 Nor cloud, nor thunder, nor lightning,
nor wind, nor water, nor air,
nor darkness, nor evening, nor morning,
nor summer, nor spring, nor heat, nor winter,

36 Nor frost, nor cold, nor hail, nor rain, nor dew,
nor noon, nor night, nor dawn, nor brightness, nor light,
save only the splendor of Elyon,
by which all shall see what is set before them.

37 For it shall endure as though by judgment only,
and it shall not move,
neither shall it be slow nor quick."

38 Then I answered and said,
"O Adonai YHWH,
behold, we are all full of sin.

39 And because of this we cannot stand before You,
nor before those who are raised.

40 And what will He do for His Name's sake?
Will He not judge according to His righteousness?"

41 And He answered me and said,

"Behold, you shall be shown the likeness of this.

42 As the farmer sows much seed upon the ground,
and plants many trees,
and yet that which is sown good in His season does not all come up,
neither does all that is planted take root,
even so it is of those who are sown in the world:
they shall not all be saved."

43 Then I answered and said,
"If I have found favor,
let me speak.

44 For if the farmer's seed do not grow up,
seeing it does not come up because it was not Your rain,
then why does one perish who was well sown?"

45 And He answered me and said,
"The seed is the word of Elohim,
and the one who sows is the Son of Man.

46 The world was created for many,
but the world to come for few."

47 Then I answered and said,
"O my soul, swallow understanding,
and devour wisdom.

48 For You have agreed to give ear,
and are willing to prophesy,
for You have no longer space than only to live."

49 And Elyon answered me, and said,
"In the beginning, when the earth was made,
before the portals of the world were fixed,
before the winds blew,
before the thunders resounded,
before the lightning shone,

50 Before the foundations of paradise were laid,
before the fair flowers were seen,
before the powers of movement were established,
and before the innumerable hosts of angels were
gathered together,

51 Before the heights of the air were lifted up,
before the measures of the firmament were named,
before the footstool of Tziyon was established,
before the present years were counted,
and before the imaginations of them that now sin was
stamped,
and before they were sealed that have gathered faith for
a treasure.

52 Then I thought upon these things,
and all were made through Me alone,
and not through another:

just as the end shall come through Me alone,
and not through another.

53 Then I answered and said,
"What shall mark the parting of the times?
Or when shall the end of the first,
and the beginning of the second, appear?"

54 And He said to me,
"From Abraham to Yitsḥaq,
when Yaʿaqov and Esau were born of him,
Yaʿaqov's hand held first the heel of Esau.

55 For Esau is the end of this age,
and Yaʿaqov is the beginning of the one that follows.

56 The hand of man is between heel and hand.
Other things, Ezra,
do not seek."

4 Ezra (2 Esdras) – Chapter 9

1 He answered me then, and said,
"Measure carefully the time diligently in itself,
and when you see that part of the signs pass,
which I have told you before,

2 Then you shall understand that it is the very time
in which Elyon is about to visit the world which He made.

3 Therefore, when there shall be seen earthquakes and
uproars of the peoples in the world,

4 Then you shall understand that Elyon spoke of those things
from the days that were before you,
even from the beginning.

5 For like as all that is made in the world has a
beginning and an end,
and the end is manifest:

6 Even so the times also of Elyon
have plain beginnings in wonder and power,
and endings in signs and marvels.

7 And every one that shall be saved,

and shall be able to escape by his works and by faith,
whereby you have believed,

8 Shall be preserved from the said perils,
and shall see My salvation in My land,
and within My borders:
for I have sanctified them for Me from the beginning.

9 Then shall they be in pitiful case,
who now have abused My ways:
and they that have cast them away despitefully,
shall dwell in torments.

10 For such as in their life have received benefits,
and have not known Me;

11 And they that have loathed My Torah,
while they still had liberty,
and, when as yet place of repentance was open to them,
understood not, but despised it;

12 The same must know it after death by pain.

13 And therefore be not curious how the ungodly shall be punished,
but inquire how the righteous shall be saved,
whose the world is,
and for whom the world was created."

14 Then I answered and said,
"I have said before, and now do speak,
and will speak it also hereafter,
that there be many more of those which perish,
than of them which shall be saved:

15 Like as a wave is greater than a drop."

16 And He answered me, saying,
"Like as the field is, so also is the seed;
as the flowers be, so are the colors also;
such as the work is, such also is the judgment;
and as the husbandman is himself,
so is his threshing-floor also.

17 For there was a time in this age,
when I was preparing for those who now live,
before the world was made for them to dwell in:
and no one spoke against Me.

18 But now the inhabitants of this world are corrupted
with wickedness,
and have so filled it with ungodliness,
that there is no longer place.

19 And as for the deeds of the righteous,
they shall be declared,
and the works of the ungodly shall be revealed."

20 So I considered the world,
and behold, it was lost;
and I saw and spared it greatly,
and have kept a grape of the cluster,
and a plant of a great people.

21 Let the multitude perish then, which was born in vain;
and let My grape be kept, and My plant:
for with great labor have I made it perfect.

22 Nevertheless, if you will let twenty more years pass,
your times shall be ended.

23 And when I had spoken these things,
I fell asleep there, and saw a vision,
and behold, there was a multitude of people in great confusion,
and the midst of them a man appeared.

24 And this man carved himself a great mountain,
and flew up upon it.

25 And I sought to see the region or place
where the mountain was carved,
and I could not.

26 After this I beheld,
and behold, all those who were gathered together

to subdue him
were greatly afraid, yet dared fight.

27 And behold, as he saw the assault of the multitude coming,
he neither lifted up hand,
nor held sword,
nor any instrument of war:

28 But only I saw how he sent out of his mouth
as it had been a blast of fire,
and out of his lips a flaming breath,
and out of his tongue he cast sparks and tempests.

29 And they were all mixed together:
the blast of fire, the flaming breath, and the great tempest,
and fell with violence upon the multitude
which was prepared to fight,
and burned them up every one,
so that suddenly of an innumerable multitude nothing was to be perceived,
but only dust and smell of smoke:
when I saw this, I was afraid.

30 After this I saw the same man come down from the mountain,
and call to him another multitude peaceable.

31 And there came many people to him,
of whom some were glad, some were sorry,
some were bound, and others brought of them that were offered.

32 Then I awoke, and behold, the dream was ended.

33 And I came into myself, and I had been troubled in spirit,
and greatly moved, and my soul was in fear.

34 And I said,
"I will declare this vision openly,
and I will make it known,
for I perceive that I have seen a vision of Elyon."

35 And I prayed to YHWH, and said,

36 "You only, O YHWH,
You only have known the depths of this mystery.

37 You have shown to Your servant this vision,
and You have made me to understand its interpretation.

38 For I know that those who are left in that time
are they that are kept by Your hand,
and that are the righteous,
because they have known You,
and have believed Your wonders.

39 And now, O YHWH,
show me also why the man whom I saw coming up
from the midst of the sea."

40 And He said to me,
"Like as no one can seek out or know
what is in the depth of the sea,
even so can no man upon earth see My Son,
or those who are with Him,
except in the time of His day.

41 This is the interpretation of the dream which you saw,
and for this you alone are enlightened.

42 For you have forsaken your own affairs,
and have applied yourself to Mine,
and have searched out My Torah.

43 For your life have you ordered in wisdom,
and have called understanding your mother.

44 And therefore I have showed you the treasures of Elyon:
after three days I will speak other things to you,
and declare to you mighty and wondrous matters."

45 Then I went my way, and gave thanks,

praising YHWH with all my heart,
because He had shown me what He promised.
And after three days I sat again,
and spoke in the same place,
and YHWH's hand was upon me.

4 Ezra (2 Esdras) – Chapter 10

1 And it happened, when I had spoken these words,
the angel who was sent to me the night before was sent again to me,

2 And said to me,
"Arise, Ezra, and hear the words that I am come to tell you."

3 And I said, "Speak on, my Adonai."
Then he said to me,

4 "There is a great multitude greater than these,
and they shall be left behind.

5 Therefore ask for yourself only,
and pray for the remnant,
for the rest of the people pray not."

6 And I wept bitterly,
and my soul was in anguish,
for I remembered the ruin of Tsion,
and the desolation of Yerushalayim.

7 And as I spoke these words,
behold, a woman appeared to me,
lamenting and mourning.

Her face was covered with ashes,
and her garments were torn,
and she was beating upon her breast with great sorrow.

8 And I said to her,
"Why are you weeping?
Why are you so grieved?"

9 And she said to me,
"Sir, let me alone that I may bewail myself,
and add to my sorrow,
for I am greatly vexed in my spirit,
and brought very low."

10 And I said to her,
"What has happened to you?
Tell me."

11 And she said to me,
"I your servant was barren,
and had no child, though I had a husband thirty years.

12 And every day and hour those thirty years
I made my prayer to Elyon,
night and day.

13 And it happened after thirty years,
Elyon heard my prayer,
and regarded my affliction,

and gave me a son.
And I rejoiced greatly with him,
I and my husband, and all my neighbors.

14 And we gave great honor to the Mighty One.

15 And I nourished him with great travail.

16 And when he grew up and came to the time that he should have a wife,
I made a feast."

17 And it happened, when my son entered his wedding chamber,
he fell down and died.

18 Then we overthrew the lights,
and all my neighbors rose up to comfort me,
and I was still very quiet until the evening of the second day.

19 And it happened, when they had all ceased to comfort me,
that I might be quiet,
then I rose up by night,
and fled, and came here into this field,
as you see.

20 And I do now purpose not to return into the city,

but to stay here,
and neither eat nor drink,
but continually to mourn and fast until I die."

21 Then I left the thoughts I had,
and answered her in anger, and said,

22 "You foolish woman above all others,
do you not see our mourning,
and what has happened to us?

23 How Tsion our mother is full of sorrow,
and humbled with much mourning,
and brought very low?

24 For since the Most High has brought upon her great sorrow,
why do you grieve for one son?

25 If you say to me,
'My lamentation is not like the earth's,
because I have lost the fruit of my womb,
which I bore with pain, and brought forth with sorrows,'

26 Let me tell you:
Tsion, the mother of us all, is full of heaviness,
and much humbled.

27 It is proper for all to mourn for her,
and to be sorrowful,
because all are in her affliction,
and all are in her pain.

28 And you grieve for one son!
Ask the earth,
and she will tell you,
that it is she who ought to mourn for the multitude she has lost,
for one spring dried up a multitude that once flowed."

29 Then I said to her,
"Hold your peace now from me,
and I will speak to you."

30 She said to me,
"Say on, my Adonai, only do not lie to me."

31 Then I said to her,
"Do not you think that the earth is better than you?
The ground bears the multitude,
but you grieve for one child.

32 Did not I say to you,
'Mourn for Tsion, because she has lost all of us,
and grieve deeply,
for we are all in her sorrow'?

33 For when I speak truth to you,
you do not believe me.
But if I speak falsehood,
you receive it lightly."

34 Then I looked,
and behold, the woman appeared no more to me,
but there was a city built,
and a great place shown from the foundations.
Then I was afraid, and cried with a loud voice, and said,

35 "Where is Uriel the angel,
who came to me at the first?
For he has caused me to fall into many trances,
and my end has turned into corruption,
and my prayer to rebuke."

36 And as I was speaking these words,
behold, he came to me,
and looked upon me.

37 And behold, I lay as one dead,
and my understanding was taken from me.
He took me by the right hand,
and comforted me,
and set me upon my feet,
and said to me,

38 "What ails you?

Why are you troubled?
Why are you so disquieted in your mind?"

39 And I said,
"Because you have forsaken me,
and yet I did according to your words.
I went into the field,
and behold, I have seen,
and yet see, what I am not able to explain."

40 He said to me,
"Stand up like a man,
and I will advise you."

41 Then I said,
"Speak on, my Adonai;
only do not forsake me, lest I die frustrated.

42 For I have seen what I did not know,
and hear what I do not understand.

43 Or is my mind deceived,
and my soul dreaming?

44 Now therefore I beseech you,
that you will show your servant the interpretation of this vision."

45 He answered me, and said,

"Listen to me, and I will instruct you,
and tell you what you fear.

46 For Elyon will reveal many secrets to you.

47 Therefore He has seen your righteous conduct,
that you have sorrowed continually for your people,
and mourned greatly for Tsion.

48 This therefore is the meaning of the vision:
The woman you saw mourning is Tsion,
which you now see as a city built.

49 And whereas she told you of the death of her son,
this is the interpretation:
This was the destruction that was about to come upon Yerushalayim.

50 And behold, you saw her likeness,
and because she mourned for her son,
you began to comfort her.
And of these things Elyon has shown you the brightness of her glory,
and the comeliness of her beauty.

51 And therefore I commanded you to remain in the field
where no foundation was built.

52 For I knew that Elyon was about to show you this.

53 Therefore I commanded you to go into the field,
where there was no building laid.

54 For in the place where Elyon will show His city,
there shall no man's building be able to stand.

55 And therefore do not be afraid,
nor let your heart be terrified,
but go in and see the beauty and greatness of the building,
as much as your eyes are able to see.

56 And then you shall hear as much as your ears may comprehend.

57 For you are blessed above many others,
and are called with Elyon,
like as only few are.

58 But tomorrow at night you shall remain here,
and Elyon shall show you visions of high things,
which He will reveal to those who dwell upon the earth
in the last days."

59 So I slept that night and the following,
as He commanded me.

4 Ezra (2 Esdras) – Chapter 11

1 Then I saw a dream,
and behold, there came up from the sea an eagle,
which had twelve feathered wings,
and three heads.

2 And I saw,
and behold, she spread her wings over all the earth,
and all the winds of the air blew upon her,
and the clouds were gathered to her.

3 And I saw,
and out of her wings there grew other little wings,
and they became small wings, but they were set up beside them.

4 And their heads were at rest:
the head in the middle was greater than the others,
yet rested with them.

5 And I saw,
and behold, the eagle flew with her wings,
to reign over the earth,
and over those who dwell in it.

6 And I saw that all things under heaven
were subject to her,

and no man spoke against her,
not even one creature upon the earth.

7 And I saw, and behold, the eagle rose upon her talons,
and spoke to her wings, saying,

8 "Do not all watch at the same time;
let every one sleep in her own place,
and watch by course.

9 But let the heads be preserved for the last."

10 And I saw, and behold, the voice did not come from her heads,
but from the middle of her body.

11 And I counted her wings,
and behold, there were eight of them on the right side,
and four on the left side.

12 And I looked,
and behold, there appeared upon her wings little wings:
and they set themselves up, one against another.

13 And it happened,
that when she reigned,
one of her heads awoke,
the one in the middle,
and it devoured the two that were with it.

14 And behold, this head put the whole earth under it,
and had power over those who dwell upon the earth,
with much oppression,
and it had greater dominion than all the wings that were past.

15 And after this I looked,
and behold, the head also died,
and there came up in her place the two heads that were left,
which reigned over the earth,
and over those who dwell in it.

16 And I saw, and behold, the head on the right
devoured the one on the left.

17 Then I heard a voice,
which said to me,
"Look before you, and consider what you see."

18 And I saw, and behold,
as it were a lion roused out of the wood, roaring,
and I heard how he sent out a man's voice to the eagle,
and spoke, saying,

19 "Hear, you, I will speak to you.
The Most High says this to you:

20 Are you not the one that remains of the four beasts,
whom I made to reign in My world,
so that the end of My times might come through them?

21 And the fourth came,
and conquered all the beasts that were past,
and had power over the world with great fear,
and over the whole compass of the earth with much wicked oppression;
and so long time dwelt he upon the earth with deceit.

22 And you have judged the earth,
but not with truth.

23 For you have afflicted the meek,
you have hurt the peaceable,
you have loved liars,
and destroyed the dwellings of those who brought forth fruit,
and cast down the walls of those who did you no harm.

24 Therefore your insolent dealing has come up to Elyon,
and your pride to the Mighty One.

25 And Elyon has looked upon His times,
and behold, they are ended,
and His ages are fulfilled.

26 And therefore appear no more, you eagle,
nor your horrible wings,
nor your wicked feathers,
nor your malicious heads,
nor your hurtful talons,
nor your wicked body,

27 That all the earth may be refreshed,
and may be relieved,
and may return, being delivered from your violence,
and that she may hope for the judgment and mercy of Him that made her."

4 Ezra (2 Esdras) – Chapter 12

1 And it happened,
while the lion spoke these words to the eagle,
I saw,

2 And behold, the head that remained
and the four wings appeared no more,
and the two wings which went over to it rose up,
and set themselves to reign,
and their kingdom was small and full of uproar.

3 And I saw,
and behold, they appeared no more,
and the whole body of the eagle was burnt,
so that the earth was greatly afraid.

4 Then I awoke out of the trouble and trance of my mind,
and from great fear,
and said to my spirit,

5 "Behold, this have You done to me,
in that You search out the ways of Elyon.

6 Behold, I am yet weary in my spirit,
and very weak in my soul;
and the vision that I have seen troubles me greatly.

7 And He said to me,
'I have showed you this dream for this cause:
because you have desired to know the secrets of Elyon.

8 Therefore this has been shown to you.
This is the interpretation of the vision:

9 The eagle whom you saw come up from the sea
is the fourth kingdom,
which appeared in a vision to your brother Daniyyel.

10 But it was not expounded to him as I now expound to you,
or have I explained it to you.

11 Behold, the days will come,
that there shall rise up a kingdom upon the earth,
and it shall be more terrible than all the kingdoms that were before it.

12 And twelve kings shall reign in it,
one after another.

13 Whereof the second shall begin to reign,
and shall have more time than any of the twelve.

14 And this is the interpretation of the twelve wings which you saw.

15 And as for the voice which you heard speak,
and that you saw not go out from the heads,
but from the middle of the body,
this is the interpretation:

16 That after the time of that kingdom there shall arise great strivings,
and it shall stand in peril of falling;
nevertheless it shall not then fall,
but shall be restored again to its first estate.

17 And whereas you saw the eight small wings sticking to her wings,
this is the interpretation:

18 That in it there shall arise eight kings,
whose times shall be short,
and their years swift.

19 And two of them shall perish:
the middle time approaching;
four shall be kept until their end approaches,
but two shall be kept to the end.

20 And whereas you saw three heads resting,
this is the interpretation:

21 In her last days shall Elyon raise up three kingdoms,

and renew many things there,
and they shall have the dominion of the earth,

22 And of those that dwell there,
with much oppression above all those that were before them.
Therefore are they called the heads of the eagle.

23 For these are they that shall accomplish her wickedness,
and that shall finish her last end.

24 And whereas you saw that the great head appeared no more,
it signifies that one of them shall die upon his bed with pain.

25 For the two that remain shall be slain with the sword.

26 For the sword of one shall devour the other:
but at the last shall he fall through the sword himself.

27 And whereas you saw two wings under the head that were over against him,
this is the interpretation:

28 These are they whom Elyon has kept to the end;
this is the small kingdom and full of trouble,
as you saw.

29 And the lion whom you saw rising up out of the wood,
and roaring, and speaking to the eagle,
and rebuking her for her unrighteousness,
with all the words which you have heard:

30 This is the Anointed One (Mashiach),
whom Elyon has kept for them and for their wickedness to the end:
He shall reprove them, and shall upbraid them with their cruelty.

31 For He shall set them alive in judgment,
and shall rebuke them, and correct them.

32 For the rest of My people shall He deliver with mercy,
those that have been preserved upon My borders,
and He shall make them joyful until the coming of the Day of Judgment,
of which I have spoken to you from the beginning.

33 This is the dream that you saw,
and this is the interpretation.

34 And you alone were worthy to know this secret of Elyon.

35 Therefore write all these things that you have seen in a book,
and hide them:

36 And teach them to the wise of your people,
whose hearts you know are able to understand and keep these secrets.

37 But wait here yourself yet seven days more,
so that you may be shown whatever it pleases Elyon to declare to you."

38 And with that he went his way.

4 Ezra (2 Esdras) – Chapter 13

1 And it happened,
after seven days,
I dreamed a dream by night:

2 And behold, there arose a wind from the sea,
that it moved all its waves.

3 And I beheld,
and behold, that Man became strong with the thousands of heaven:
and when He turned His countenance to look,
all the things trembled that were seen under Him.

4 And whenever the voice went out of His mouth,
all they burned that heard His voice,
like as the earth fails when it feels the fire.

5 And after this I beheld,
and behold, there was gathered together a multitude of men,
out of number, from the four winds of the heaven,
to subdue the Man that came out of the sea.

6 But I beheld,
and behold, He had graven Himself a great mountain,
and flew up upon it.

7 But I would have seen the region or place
where the hill was graven,
and I could not.

8 And after this I beheld,
and behold, all they which were gathered together to subdue Him
were greatly afraid,
and yet dared fight.

9 And behold, as He saw the violence of the multitude that came,
He neither lifted up His hand,
nor held sword,
nor any instrument of war:

10 But only I saw that He sent out of His mouth
as it had been a blast of fire,
and out of His lips a flaming breath,
and out of His tongue He cast out sparks and tempests.

11 And they were all mixed together:
the blast of fire, the flaming breath,
and the great tempest,
and fell with violence upon the multitude,
which was prepared to fight,
and burned them up every one,
so that upon a sudden of an innumerable multitude,

nothing was to be perceived,
but only dust and smell of smoke:
when I saw this, I was afraid.

12 Afterward I saw the same Man come down from the mountain,
and call to Him another multitude peaceable.

13 And there came many people to Him,
whereof some were glad,
some were sorry,
some of them were bound,
and others brought of them that were offered.

14 Then was I sick through great fear,
and I awoke, and said,

15 "You have shown Your servant these wonders from the beginning,
and have counted me worthy that You should receive my prayer:

16 Yet show me now also the interpretation of this dream.

17 For as I conceive in my understanding,
woe to those that shall be left in those days;
and much more woe to those that are not left behind!

18 For they that were not left were in heaviness.

19 Now I understand those things which are laid up in the latter days,
which shall happen to them,
and to those that are left behind.

20 Therefore are they come into great perils
and many necessities,
like as these dreams declare.

21 Yet it is easier for him that is in danger to come into these things,
than to pass away as a cloud out of the world,
and not to see the things that happen in the last days."

22 And He answered to me, and said,
"This is the interpretation of the vision:

23 The Man whom you saw rising up from the heart of the sea,
is He whom Elyon has kept a great season,
which by His own Self shall deliver His creation:
and He shall order them that are left behind.

24 And whereas you saw that out of His mouth
there came a blast of wind, and fire, and storm;

25 And that He held neither sword, nor any instrument of war,
but that the rushing in of Him destroyed the multitude that came to fight against Him:
this is the interpretation:

26 Behold, the days come,
when Elyon will begin to deliver those that are upon the earth.

27 And He shall come to the astonishment of those that dwell on the earth.

28 And one shall undertake to fight against another,
one city against another,
one place against another,
one people against another,
and one realm against another.

29 And the time shall be,
when these things shall come to pass,
and the signs shall happen which I showed you before,
then shall My Son be declared,
whom you saw as a Man rising from the sea.

30 And when all the people hear His voice,
every man shall in their own land leave the battle
they have against one another.

31 And an innumerable multitude shall be gathered together,
as you saw them,
willing to come, and to overcome Him by fighting.

32 But He shall stand upon the top of Mount Tsion.

33 And Tsion shall come,
and shall be shown to all men,
being prepared and built,
like as you saw the hill graven without hands.

34 And this My Son shall rebuke the wicked inventions of those nations,
which for their wicked life are fallen into the tempest;

35 And shall lay before them their evil thoughts,
and the torments wherewith they shall begin to be tormented,
which are like to a flame:
and He shall destroy them without labor by the Torah, which is like to fire.

36 And whereas you saw Him gather another peaceable multitude to Him;

37 Those are the ten tribes,
which were carried away prisoner out of their own land in the time of Hoshea the king,

whom Shalmaneser the king of Assyria led away captive,
and he carried them over the waters,
and so came they into another land.

38 But they took this counsel among themselves,
that they would leave the multitude of the nations,
and go forth into a further country,
where never mankind dwelt,

39 That they might there keep their statutes,
which they never kept in their own land.

40 And they entered into Euphrates by the narrow passages of the river.

41 For Elyon then showed signs for them,
and held still the flood,
till they were passed over.

42 For through that country there was a great way to go,
namely of a year and a half:
and the same region is called Arsareth.

43 Then they dwelt there until the latter time;
and now when they shall begin to come,

44 Elyon shall hold still the springs of the stream again,
that they may go through:

therefore you saw the multitude with peace.

45 But those that be left behind of your people,
are they that are found within My holy borders.

46 Now when He destroys the multitude of the nations
that are gathered together,
He shall defend His people that remain.

47 And then shall He show them very many wonders."

48 Then I said,
"O YHWH Adonai,
show me this: why have I seen the Man coming up from
the midst of the sea?"

49 And He said to me,
"Like as no man can seek out or know what is in the
depths of the sea,
so no man upon earth can see My Son,
or those that be with Him,
except in the time of His day.

50 This is the interpretation of the dream which you
saw,
and you alone are enlightened in this.

51 For you have forsaken your own matters,
and applied yourself to Mine,

and searched out My Torah;

52 For your life have you ordered in wisdom,
and have called understanding your mother.

53 Therefore have I shown you the treasures of Elyon:
after another three days I will speak other things to you,
and declare to you mighty and wondrous things."

54 Then I awoke, and I blessed Elyon,
and gave thanks to Him that had dealt so wondrously with me,
and I said,

55 "Blessed be Your Name, O YHWH,
Elohim of our fathers,
who has appointed me to knowledge,
and to reveal to me the deep and hidden things
of Your wonders."

4 Ezra (2 Esdras) – Chapter 14

1 And it happened upon the third day,
I sat under an oak,
and behold, a voice came out of a bush over against me,
and said, "Ezra, Ezra."

2 And I said, "Here I am, YHWH."
And I stood up upon my feet.

3 Then He said to me,
"I revealed Myself in a bush,
and spoke to Moshe,
when My people served in Mitsrayim.

4 And I sent him,
and led My people out of Mitsrayim,
and brought him up to Mount Sinai,
and kept him by Me many days.

5 And told him many wondrous things,
and showed him the secrets of the times,
and the end;
and commanded him, saying,

6 'These words shall you declare,
and these shall you hide.'

7 And now I say to you, Ezra:
Lay up in your heart the signs that I have shown,
and the dreams that you have seen,
and the interpretations which you have heard:

8 For you shall be taken away from among men,
and from henceforth you shall remain with My Son,
and with such as be like you,
until the times be ended.

9 For the world has lost its youth,
and the times begin to wax old.

10 For the world is divided into twelve parts,
and the ten parts of it are gone already,
and half of a tenth part:

11 And there remains that which is after the half of the tenth part."

12 Now therefore set your house in order,
and reprove your people,
comfort the lowly among them,
and instruct those that be wise;
and now renounce corruption,
let go from your mortal thoughts,
cast away the burdens of man,
put off now the weak nature,

13 And set aside the thoughts that are most heavy to you,
and haste to flee from these times.

14 For yet greater evils than those which you have seen happen
shall be done hereafter.

15 For look how much the world shall be weaker through age,
so much the more shall evils increase upon them that dwell there.

16 For the truth is fled far away,
and falsehood is hard at hand:
for now the vision to come is hastening,
and shall not pass away.

17 But if I have lived,
yet will I speak these things with you,
O YHWH:

18 Behold, I will go, as You have commanded me,
and reprove the people which are present:
but they that shall be born afterward,
who shall admonish them?
Thus the world is set in darkness,
and they that dwell there are without light.

19 For Your Torah is burned,
therefore no man knows the things that are done of You,
or the work that shall begin.

20 But if I have found favor before You,
send the Ruach ha'Qodesh into me,
and I shall write all that has been done in the world
since the beginning,
which were written in Your Torah,
that men may find Your path,
and that they which will live in the latter days may live."

21 And He answered me, saying,
"Go your way, gather the people together,
and say to them,
that they seek you not for forty days.

22 But look you prepare many writing tablets,
and take with you Sarea, Dabria, Selemia, Ethanus, and Asiel,
these five who are ready to write swiftly.

23 And come here, and I shall light a candle of understanding in your heart,
which shall not be put out,
till the things are performed which you shall begin to write.

24 And when you have finished,
some things you shall publish,
and some things you shall deliver in secret to the wise:
tomorrow this hour shall you begin to write."

25 Then went I forth,
as He commanded me,
and gathered all the people together,
and said,

26 "Hear these words, O Yisra'el:

27 Our fathers at the beginning were strangers in Mitsrayim,
from whence they were delivered:

28 And received the Torah of life,
which they kept not,
which you also have transgressed after them.

29 Then was the land, even the land of Tsion, given you for a possession:
but you yourselves, and your fathers, have done unrighteousness,
and have not kept the ways which the Most High commanded you.

30 And because He is a righteous Judge,

He took from you in time the thing that He had given you.

31 And now are you here,
and your brethren among you.

32 Therefore, if so be, that you will subdue your own understanding,
and reform your hearts,
you shall be kept alive,
and after death you shall obtain mercy.

33 For after death shall the judgment come,
when we shall live again:
and then shall the names of the righteous be manifest,
and the works of the wicked shall be declared.

34 Let no man therefore come to me now,
nor seek after me these forty days."

35 So I took the five men,
as He commanded me,
and we went into the field,
and remained there.

36 And the next day, behold,
a voice called me, saying,
"Ezra, open your mouth,
and drink that I give you to drink."

37 Then opened I my mouth,
and behold, He reached me a full cup,
which was full as it were with water,
but the color of it was like fire.

38 And I took it, and drank:
and when I had drunk of it,
my heart uttered understanding,
and wisdom grew in my breast,
for my Ruach kept memory:

39 And my mouth was opened and shut no more.

40 The Most High gave understanding
to the five men,
and they wrote the wonderful visions of the night
which were told, which they knew not:

41 And they sat forty days,
and wrote in the daytime,
and at night they ate bread.

42 As for me, I spoke in the day,
and I held not my tongue by night.

43 In forty days they wrote two hundred and four books.

44 And it happened,
when the forty days were fulfilled,
that Elyon spoke, saying,
"The first that you have written publish openly,
that the worthy and unworthy may read it:

45 But keep the seventy last,
that you may deliver them only to such as be wise
among the people:

46 For in them is the spring of understanding,
the fountain of wisdom,
and the stream of knowledge."

47 And I did so.

Appendix Notes: Key Terms & Images in Ezra

These notes are included to help readers understand key images and terms within Ezra's visions. They are not interpretations added to the text, but explanations drawn from Hebrew thought and Scripture, to bring clarity to those seeking to understand YHWH's revelation.

Note on "the Sea" (Chapter 13)
In Hebrew thought, "the sea" is often symbolic of the nations or the deep waters of chaos (see Isaiah 17:12–13, Daniel 7:3, Revelation 13:1).
This vision does not mean Messiah literally rises out of the ocean. It means He will suddenly arise out of the nations to be revealed to the whole world.
The abyss is also associated with the depths (Luke 8:31), which is why demons fear being cast there.
This image points to the suddenness of His appearing and His authority over all creation, including the abyss.

Note on the Word "Son"
In Hebrew, the word ben (son) means more than just a male child.
It can mean an expression, a representative, or one who carries the nature of another.
When YHWH calls Yeshua "My Son," He is revealing that Yeshua is His own visible Manifestation. He is not a

another being or a separate Elohim, but YHWH Himself made known to humanity.

Note on "Most High" (Elyon)
The title Elyon means "Most High" and emphasizes YHWH's absolute supremacy over every power, earthly or spiritual.
When Ezra cries out to Elyon, he is appealing to the One above all nations, rulers, angels, and principalities.
This title reassures the reader that no force of darkness or empire can rival YHWH's authority.

Note on "Days Are Shortened" (Chapters 4 and 7)
When Ezra is told the days will be shortened, this does not simply mean that time will move faster. It means YHWH will limit the days of judgment so that His chosen ones are not completely destroyed.
Yeshua echoes this in Matthew 24:22: "For the sake of the elect those days will be cut short."
This is a sign of mercy, showing that even in wrath, YHWH remembers His people.

Note on "The Eagle" and "The Lion" (Chapters 11–12)
The eagle represents the world's oppressive kingdoms, culminating in the final empire that opposes YHWH's people.
The lion who arises from the forest is the Messiah, the Lion of the Tribe of Judah, who confronts the eagle, rebukes its arrogance, and brings final justice.

This is one of the clearest Messianic prophecies outside the Torah and Prophets. It reveals Yeshua's role as the Judge of the nations.

Note on "Fire" and "Flame" (Chapter 13)
When Ezra sees fire and storm proceeding from the figure, this is not mere destruction but a picture of divine purity.
Fire in Hebrew thought represents the Presence of YHWH (Exodus 3:2, Hebrews 12:29). It consumes what is wicked and refines what is righteous.
This vision shows Yeshua's return as both Warrior and Purifier of the earth.

Glossary of Names and Terms in 4 Ezra
(2 Esdras 3–14)

Adam (אָדָם)
The first man, formed by YHWH from the dust of the ground. Given the breath of life, but transgressed the command and brought death into the generations after him. Ezra frequently recalls Adam as the root of human sin and mortality.

Adonai (אֲדֹנָי)
Title meaning "Master" or "Lord," used in prayer to acknowledge YHWH's sovereign authority.

Babylon (בָּבֶל)
The city of exile where Ezra and the people of Yisra'el lived after the destruction of the Second Temple. Symbol of worldly power and idolatry in contrast to the holiness of Tsion.

David (דָּוִד)
The king chosen by YHWH to establish His Name in Yerushalayim. Ezra recalls David as one who built the city where incense and offerings were presented to YHWH.

Elohim (אֱלֹהִים)

Hebrew for "Mighty One(s)." Used in Scripture to refer to YHWH, but also at times to false gods, angelic beings, or human rulers depending on context. In Ezra, preserved where original manuscripts indicate.

Esau (עֵשָׂו)

The elder twin of Ya'aqov. Rejected in favor of Ya'aqov, symbolizing YHWH's sovereign election of His covenant people.

Eternal Torah of Life (תּוֹרַת חַיִּים)

Phrase in Ezra referring to YHWH's instruction as the way of life given to His people. Highlights the covenant path contrasted with the wicked heart of mankind.

Elyon (עֶלְיוֹן)

Title meaning "Most High." Used frequently in Ezra as the supreme designation of YHWH.

Ezra (עֶזְרָא)

The scribe, prophet, and intercessor who laments before YHWH after the destruction of the Temple. Receives visions and revelations through the angel Uriel, questioning divine justice and the fate of mankind.

Israel (יִשְׂרָאֵל)

The chosen people of YHWH, descendants of Ya'aqov. In Ezra, their sins and punishments are contrasted with the apparent prosperity of the nations.

Jacob / Ya'aqov (יַעְקֹב)

Son of Yitshaq, chosen by YHWH over Esau. Father of the twelve tribes of Israel. Ezra recalls the covenant blessings flowing through him.

Moshe (מֹשֶׁה)

The prophet who led Israel out of Egypt and received the Torah on Mount Sinai. In Ezra, remembered as the one through whom YHWH gave the law.

Mount Sinai (הַר סִינַי)

The mountain where YHWH descended in glory and gave the Torah to Israel amid fire, earthquake, wind, and frost.

Noah (נֹחַ)

Righteous man preserved through the flood with his household. In Ezra, seen as a symbol of YHWH's mercy amidst judgment.

Ruach (רוּחַ)

The Spirit of YHWH. The breath, wind, and presence of the Most High at work in creation and revelation.

Torah (תּוֹרָה)

Instruction or law given by YHWH to His people. In Ezra, presented both as gift and as unfulfilled because of mankind's wicked heart.

Tsion / Zion (צִיּוֹן)

The holy city chosen by YHWH for His dwelling. Desolate in Ezra's day yet destined for restoration.

Uriel (אוּרִיאֵל)

The angelic messenger sent by YHWH to answer Ezra's questions. His name means "El is my light." He delivers visions, explanations, and mysteries of the end times.

Yeshua (יֵשׁוּעַ)

The revealed identity of YHWH in the flesh. Preserved in the restoration as the fullness of His salvation, though not named directly in Ezra, His presence is revealed in the promises of mercy and future deliverance.

YHWH (יהוה)

The covenant Name of the Most High, restored wherever later manuscripts obscured it with "Lord" or "God." The One who spoke creation, gave Torah, and revealed mysteries to Ezra.

Yitshaq (יִצְחָק)

Son of Avraham, father of Ya'aqov and Esau. Remembered in Ezra as the heir of covenant promises.

References & Sources

The following manuscripts and scholarly works were consulted in preparing this restoration. They represent the earliest surviving witnesses to 4 Ezra (2 Esdras) and critical studies that have preserved its integrity across centuries. They are cited here so that every reader may discern for themselves the foundation upon which this restoration has been faithfully undertaken.

Primary Manuscripts & Witnesses
Latin Codex Sangermanensis I (9th century), Bibliothèque nationale de France, Paris.
Latin Codex Ambrosianus (9th century), Biblioteca Ambrosiana, Milan.
Surviving Syriac manuscripts (6th–7th century), preserved in Eastern Christian traditions.
Ethiopic (Ge'ez) manuscripts, transmitted through the Ethiopian Orthodox Church.

Critical Editions & Scholarly Collections
Charles, R.H. The Apocrypha and Pseudepigrapha of the Old Testament. Oxford: Clarendon Press, 1913.
Charlesworth, James H., ed. The Old Testament Pseudepigrapha. 2 vols. New Haven: Yale University Press, 1983–1985.
Stone, Michael E. Fourth Ezra: A Commentary on the Book of Fourth Ezra. Minneapolis: Fortress Press, 1990.

Metzger, Bruce M. An Introduction to the Apocrypha. New York: Oxford University Press, 1957.

Secondary Studies & Linguistic Tools
Bogaert, Pierre-Maurice. Esdras: Introduction et commentaire. Sources chrétiennes. Paris: Éditions du Cerf, 1979.
Hanhart, Robert. Text and Transmission of 4 Ezra. Göttingen: Septuaginta-Unternehmen.
Brown, Francis, S.R. Driver, and Charles A. Briggs. A Hebrew and English Lexicon of the Old Testament (BDB). Oxford: Clarendon Press, 1906.
Bauer, Walter, Frederick W. Danker, William F. Arndt, and F. Gingrich. A Greek-English Lexicon of the New Testament and Other Early Christian Literature (BDAG). 3rd ed. Chicago: University of Chicago Press, 2000.
Standard interlinear Bible tools: Hebrew, Greek, and Latin concordances (various critical editions).

Comparative Sources
Dead Sea Scrolls fragments (for parallel Hebraic concepts, though not containing Ezra directly).
Septuagint (LXX), for comparative Greek renderings of Hebraic thought.
Masoretic Text (MT), for continuity of covenant language across the Tanakh.
Lexicons and interlinear concordances for restored divine names and Hebraic thought-forms.

Restoration Principle

Where manuscripts diverged, preference was given to the readings most faithful to the Hebraic thought patterns, style, and covenant identity of YHWH. Later insertions or doctrinal expansions were acknowledged but not adopted into the restored text.

About the Sacred Writings Restoration Project

This volume is part of the ongoing Sacred Writings Project, a labor dedicated to recovering and restoring the unaltered Word of YHWH. Many books once read, honored, and preserved by the faithful were later removed or obscured, not by divine command, but by human councils, empires, and institutions.

The purpose of this project is not to invent, reinterpret, or impose personal bias. It is to restore what was rightfully given: sacred writings that testify of YHWH, reveal His covenant, and proclaim Yeshua as YHWH made visible. Books such as Enoch, 2 Esdras, Baruch, Jubilees, and others will be carefully restored, not because of novelty or preference, but because of their rightful place in bearing witness to the Most High and His dealings with His creation.

These writings are considered sacred and holy because they were entrusted to prophets, scribes, and seers by YHWH Himself. They carry the weight of His revelation, preserved not by human will, but by the Spirit who ensures His Word is never fully lost. Where men erased or altered, YHWH preserved a remnant for His people.

The restorer of this work does not stand under the rule of any denomination, institution, or church. She fears no council of men, but fears YHWH alone. Every decision in this restoration has been made with reverence before Him, not for approval by human systems. It is for this reason that His Name and His Word are restored here without compromise and without malice. This restoration is not done to oppose men, nor to seek recognition, but only to return to the unaltered Word entrusted to the remnant of YHWH.

Furthermore, this restoration is one step in that unfolding work. As with all that is holy, the invitation is simple: test everything before YHWH Himself. If these words carry His breath, they will bear fruit in the hearts of those who seek Him.

May all who read be strengthened, awakened, and returned to the covenant of YHWH Yeshua.

www.ingramcontent.com/pod-product-compliance
Lightning Source LLC
Chambersburg PA
CBHW020341010526
44119CB00048B/556